The Siren Sonnets

poems by

Cindy Bosley

Finishing Line Press
Georgetown, Kentucky

The Siren Sonnets

ACKNOWLEDGMENTS

"Siren, Jealous" first appeared in *Flyway Literary Review,* Spring 1996, as "You
Don't Have to Leave the Room."

"In Siren's Bedroom" first appeared in *Pathways: Literary and Arts Journal of
Owens Community College,* Spring 1999.

Special thanks to Sheryl St. Germain for being Teacher in the most important
ways.

And a most delightedly-special thanks to my writing group which includes
Leonard Kress, Carl Dietrich, Joy Parker, and Shannon Smith of our decades-
long writing workshop. You have been astonishing and steadfast writing and
muse-driven partners, and every one of these poems shines a little extra because
of your input.

My thanks and my love to Todd Hickman.

Publisher: Leah Maines
Editor: Christen Kincaid
Cover Art: Emma Bosley-Smith
Author Photo: Cynthia Bosley
Cover Design: Elizabeth Maines

Printed in the USA on acid-free paper.
Order online: www.finishinglinepress.com
        also available on amazon.com

Author inquiries and mail orders:
Finishing Line Press
P. O. Box 1626
Georgetown, Kentucky 40324
U. S. A.

Table of Contents

This book is dedicated to my three astonishing daughters, Emma, Isabel, and Molly.

Desire is the source of all suffering.
—Buddha

Siren and Her Sisters Eating Mulberries

We stabbed ourselves at the tops of trees.
Berries left hickeys on our knees
and bright-blood kisses on our smothered arms.

To play the game, we had to climb the arbor
to eat from the biting tree. We had to kiss
the tree queen.

In the depths of the mulberry
outbuildings, we heard our mothers
screaming from inside the jungle

of the house. We stayed away and sweetened
each other with kicking and biting.
When the wind blew, we became the trees

and we could not hear our mothers, and nothing
could hurt us, and all of us could sing.

Siren Waiting

"That man who unsuspecting approaches them, and listens
to the Sirens' singing, has no hope of coming home."
—Homer's Odyssey

As they fight being dashed against the rocks,
I wait for them to venture closer here,
their bent mouths, red and raven and blonde locks,
their eyes for subtle love, the softest beards

upon my cheek, imaginary things:
men tied with braided rays of morning sun.
From my lonely bed, a rich voice sings
one song, my throaty tenor tremulous

as a breeze-shivered meadow near a stream.
Windless calm falls there; a divinity
spoils my unclean wish to hold them. Heartless
beats the oversaturated heart in me.

Reason, like brisk air, sets them back at sail
and, freed, they celebrate that I failed.

Siren's Prayer

"Then we die with our eyes open, if we are going to die,
or know what death we baffle if we can."
—Odysseus, Homer's Odyssey

Nights find me calculating ways to snag
ashore the handsome sailors. I admire
those men, explorers of the tricky sea.

They would drown because of me.
It's never been my wish for them to die
so far from home, it's just what they inspire.

My heart has been remiss to think
my love's returned; for all my lust,
my lovers go home and I am spurned.

Forbidden sex denies the flesh
from which the night is built. Complex
scaffolding and handmade skies complete

with balconies permit my view of them:
faithful ones I both covet and condemn.

The Request

"You must tie me fast with even more lashings."
—Homer's Odyssey

They think I don't hear them, but I hear them.
Hurriedly bundling up their ropes and ties,
they warm the wax to save their ears from harm.
One man steadfastly bound against his cries

holds on despite desire. It's him I want,
though he's one of many whose eyes feast
upon my golden shoulders. Bare, I flaunt
and foist my eager voice across the seas.

I wrap my weighty breasts till he is near
enough to jump; if he would leap to me
I'd forget all wicked songs; he'd then hear
true sounds in my voice. Look, his quiet beauty

sheds my resolve. "Odysseus, spend an hour
upon these lips; come willingly ashore."

Siren's Naughty Dream

"Are you flesh and blood, Odysseus, to endure more than a man can?
Do you never tire?"
              —Homer's Odyssey

I dreamed last night. Heroes waited aboard
their straining ship, harbor-anchored, while my
sisters took their turns sleeping on the floor.
And what charms lay under blankets! Goodbye,

to singing from afar. There's a hero
who knows my pleasures beyond song. I've touched
beneath their gowns in night's darkness. They call
my passionate name, Ligeia, bright-voiced.

My would-be lover rhymes his lips with cheek
with hair, and captain's hands. These lost dreams keep
returning with strong storms, yet I remain
alone, thinking, "A dream. No harm or blame,"

but others have seen my sinful visions:
dreams, for me, have always been intentions.

Siren Contemplates Her Nature

> *"It is they, who by their own recklessness win sorrow*
> *beyond what is given."*
> —Homer's *Odyssey*

I yearn; for hardened men upon the sea.
I recognize a certain loneliness
in spirit upon the boat. I'm angry
my invitations cause so much distress.

I think I've not always been a Siren;
I remember certain ripe moments from my
life before: I believe I lay with men
who didn't die in my arms. I'm unsure,

now, about what's real. He seems quite real.
The good man holds fast against my guile,
and I can see he wants no part. Yet, I'd steal
that vast heart of his away all the while

he only dreams of me. He sleeps through
the rocking waves. I moan; it knocks him free.

In Siren's Bedroom

> *"Nor did the heart in me wish to go on living any longer*
> *nor to look on the sunlight."*
> —Homer's *Odyssey*

My nightmares come in couplets, solitude
a drowsy companion that can't comfort
nor rock me back to sleep. I knead the hurt
away as I can. Who would intrude

at these late hours? My hero has moved past
the shores, past the cliffs, past my luring pleas
while sun settles on these shoulders, at last,
despite hunger, urgency, unease.

My pillows smell of the meadow's ripe leaves
and I've woven myself a drape of raw
wool to bed down, alone. The one I need
now is absent. My many visions draw

him forward, beyond troubled sea and ship;
this heart beckons his soul; I let drop my slip.

Siren, Jealous

"My love, how wonderful to have lived while you lived."
—Richard Jackson

I can't help thinking of the women you were
never with, but loved
in libraries, hospitals, crowded basements
at parties, and in other countries.

I dread those women you don't allow yourself
to touch. You run away, mutter apologies in secret.
I think that when they catalogue old lovers,
you're at the top, shimmering fingers, eyes.

In dreams at night, you come back to them.
Their wishes on those nights: music, rain.
I don't need to know about contritenesses
with you, what you thought but didn't do.

You don't have to leave the room. Stay, kiss me.
Like them, I spend the night thinking what it might be like.

Harpie, Saddened, Surveys the Damage

"Sweet coupled airs we sing...like honey twining."
—Homer's Odyssey

I see men's bodies crushed on rocks below,
I see the lost expressions in their eyes,
I saw them flung from homeward ships, thrown
like willing bodies toward my voice that cried

atop the boulders meant to catch the swell
of spraying water. Like fevered fish who swim
too far inland, they founder. Meaningless: to dwell
upon these lost ones. Though I gaze at them,

cold hours can't help me beyond my grief.
One of them has fought a while, ropes still tied
'round his wrists and waist—it's him. I believe
I courted him this distance to drink wine

and dance. Perhaps shared comfort through the night,
but watch: his nimble ship sinks past my sight.

Siren Walks the Stones

Sailors, I sing you separately
and collectively like students. Or judges.
Music softens my choking.
Surely, you know now
how the body's cloth holds up.
Does the wide space tighten? Are you dry?

Do you miss me? Music softens my choking.
I cannot visit your graves,
don't want to see your stones,
though I walk on stones every day.
I choke when the music softens.
I watched you move, you who know now
how we are judged, and how sweetly
heavenly music chokes.

Siren's Unrest through Winter

Snow and sparrows arrive at the same time.
My cat trills in the window at the thought,
"They could all be mine!" The other cat climbs
the curtains and the chair. My desire's caught

like a cat in the rafters. My want
sings. Like a whippoorwill, it asks for things:
want to ride a horse, want milk. Undaunted,
apples, please, come here; swim to me. Stirrings

without source, like a child in my belly.
Somewhere in a public park, two people
cling, unafraid of being seen. My jealousy
lies like a feline, warm, without purpose.

Knitting lamb's wool, I avoid my choices.
Where's my Love? We'd give each other voices.

Siren as Working Class

Rotting Spring air comes through the long
hot Summer. The stench of a flowering tree
should be beautiful, but smells, instead, of the sea;
fish and brine-soaked beach and water remain

a glimmer of hope for the locals. If only
they were content as local people.
If only they had no dreams of travel,
no bills to count in wallets toward a train ticket

they can't afford. Honor's at stake, muscular strength
and factory jobs, or worse: the greasy work of cars.
Like Midwestern Sisyphus deep in toil and repetition,
holding up the stone, then free, then holding up the stone,

it's clear they watch the tight smiles of those who
have everything and cannot bear being hated for it.

The Seduction

It happens this way: I float toward him,
a glider, my wings fully spread. I hover
where he is bound upright, then make a circle
ten times or so, intent upon my lover.

He is Leda to my Swan, a sweet
fantasy I've kept from my cold sisters.
His men stand in wonder, transfixed like sheep
upon my opal wings. The first kisses

are private. I drape him as I descend,
and wrap my limbs, not gently, round the mast.
I untie twine binding his willing hands.
Into me, I take his mouth (his laughter

escapes) and the rest of him. Our aria
carries to shore in waves, crashing hard.

Odysseus Sits with the Maiden

> *"...and her hands had grown so unused to marriage that the god's*
> *infinitely gentle touch of guidance hurt her, like an undesired kiss."*
> —Homer's *Odyssey*

The manner of my hands upon my lap
discloses shyness and stills the long gaze
which passes between us, pressure rising

into a gust of notes. I long to raise
these skirts to pleasure, lace up shoes that tap
a modest rhythm, feel his song's surprise.

I keep certain pictures of him smiling,
holding his guitar, or is it a lyre?
and strumming. He sings of cities and love-
making. My heart closes eyes and skips breath.

Inside his voice, I feel water swell while his deft
fingers trail down the belly of my thigh.
His eyes mix potions strong enough to move
the strange, uneasy measure of my sighing.

Siren Breaks the Winter Solo

I wait for a right moment to light the candle.
With half a foot of snow and the distant ships,
I have to find a way to live. The prairie beyond me
is wide and white, and I think of running.

I try not to want things I've surrendered.
Tonight, I'll say prayers for the sailors and ships.
Not for what I want, but for someone's will.
The night mews like a feline stretched out for a duration.

I'm sure I'm the only one watching the brilliance
of the sea lions on their beach. I'm a young sea lion,
and I'll suckle from anything. I'll sacrifice and hunt.
Careful of the music, careful to step around the dirge,

carefully step to mark a grave with a stick and stone,
a stretch of wire to mark where I mourn.

Siren's Temptation Sonnet

> *"Why didn't I, from the full, beloved face*
> *as I raised it to my lips, why didn't I drink*
> *world, so near that I could almost taste it?*
>
> *Ah, I drank. Insatiably I drank."*
> —R.M. Rilke, "World was in the face of the beloved"

It is too close to discuss,
this new feeling, offensively arisen
like the bribing sun wandering
in off the street to take a good look
at everything, the sun who would pay
to be able to remain.

Does he dream about me?
He does. His tender-touching fingers
stay all night on my shoulder,
asking to disrobe, lustful and eager
to cut short the wishes of flesh. Hear
a faint trumpet, played by a sailor
growing closer, as if the animate coils
of sound could enter me, once released.

Sailor in the Rapunzel Garden

Rapunzel shields itself deep in the sunflower garden
of the queen witch. The empty womb's on our side of the fence,
and glorious water pools just out of reach. The witch's wicked eyes
seep, gleeful for rich neighbors who are tense to get richer,

and have sent my sailor out for fish. My pregnancy grows:
others watch from windows. The sailor says goodbye. His fingers
hook the fishing net mesh, and then the mending's done.
His boat unmoors, the cooler is packed with beer, snacks, steaks.

I wrap the net around its pole and do whatever he has ever said:
rough tailor in a risky beard and flannel shirt. His farewell fingers
do the work of spiders across my skin. Heavy green leaves
around my feet cloak the secretive stems and dirt, these plants

which have no trouble flowering, accepting without thought
the elements of the season: garden's blossom and shipyard's open rot.

Siren as a Housewife

I want clarity that comes from folding
sheets. I spend my afternoons hanging clothes
on the closet door and doing my dishwashing
in the grey wash-water. Socks leap, their toes

dark, they leap from the basket and push like
children against my calves and knees. Static
snaps as do weaker twigs of autumn oak
trees. I sway under a world of chores: brick

to scour, wool blankets to billow and air,
floral pillowcases to iron, clean, and shuck
with these disappointed hands. Hear it? There,
running the house's boundaries, ducts

carry quiet stores of grief. Someone's shoes
wait, shined and paired, still-boxed, nearly new.

Siren's Laryngitis

"She had satisfied all her desire with weeping."
—Homer's Odyssey

I have satisfied all my desire
with weeping. As drowning seamen lure me
from the meadow's bounds: these burning iris,
frank daisy, and pink opium poppies

halo my head in colorful chains. The flutes
and village musicians' carved wooden horns
bear aloft my jealousies for beauties
of the town. Veiled harlots ignore my scorn

and devour tales as the hero dashes
my good name with strumming. We're rumored
together, bed of skulls, when his ship crashed
at the water's edge near my home. In humor,

his tales are told. Good faith or not, they'll hear
Truth: my song was refused. He disappeared.

Postcard from the Siren

Friday night, almost 5.
I miss you, but it's not clear:
your face. I'm thinking
of the forest we didn't venture into.

If I got paid for just one thing,
like a prostitute in the capital,
I wouldn't fear the dark.

I found a birdhouse
wedged into the fence and dumped
its rainwater in the yard.

My near-successes. I'm on
vacation. I wake shaking,
then still. Giving up sports.
Think I'll stick to singing.

Siren Hears Someone Else's Song

"Oh you vile gods, in jealousy supernatural!
You hate it when we choose to lie with
men—immortal flesh by some dear mortal side."
—Homer's Odyssey

When his voice emerged undressed, the morning
vibrated, ripe and uncontrolled as the sun.
That star appeared to dangle near, then drift, like un-
done lace, his song arriving clear, and growing

more complex. My turn came: my throat without
speech as his eyes breathed their lonely letters,
and his voice opened. Carefully etched regret
in packages of notes meandered down

until I couldn't move for listening.
At the foot of a mountain of smooth bones
we almost met, nearly collided, but loans,
the spirit's debts, unpaid and outstanding,

had no mercy: although he had the grace
to leave me, music lingered in his place.

Siren's Pregnancy, the Last Day

No such love as yours ever tore me open,
and now she's almost here.
The last days have been sad,
waiting for it to be over;

the long months make me cry.
My brain is a tulip of unfortunate events:
closed up when it gets too cold. Night comes.
Day—open, rain.

I want my mother to tell the story again:
my father had a date the night I was born.
Beautiful things have flaws. Love resides
in my stomach, a late spring.

She doesn't want to come out. She wants
to lie inside, feel your fingers through my skin: so close.

Siren Calls In Sick

"The goddesses stayed home for shame."
—Homer's Odyssey

Something's gone awry.
I can't bear to sing again
to ships of swarthy men
who'd crash upon my coast.

My breast now unwilling
to harbor more sailors, good men
no match for these serenades.
My sisters and I adore them;

we ache to see the ships' pale masts
glide through our corridor. But just
one soul keeps me home this lonely hour.
The gale-strong illness which oppresses—

my heartbreak and heavy shame—
when love ends, they feel the same.

Siren at Yoga

"For there is strong compulsion upon me."
—Homer's *Odyssey*

If I added together these tortures,
the sum would be great; as much as his eyes
yield, as many as the twenty times my lures
failed, I see he loves me, but still, he shies

away. I am patient, pretending there's
room for hope. I address, sometimes, the air:
"Odysseus, toss me any careless kiss
sailing lonely." My heart remains unclear

about certain cruel matters. For instance,
"Whose graceful arms wrap you upon dry land,
whose hair trails your sea-tanned chest? Whose glance
brings you, begging, ashore?" Please understand,

I'm the pixie of this meadow, unkempt
and bird-wild. My wings hang lovely though clipped.

The Marriage

Three or four years
since his heavenly boat

sailed, our chances gone,
my memory is still tied by ropes.

A raspy tautness
ratchets at my throat.

I cannot help but try, still, to sing.
He whispered adoration, hope,

and touched me in such
rhythms. Our love lived, remote

but unrevised, and sweet
as summer lilies which float

the inland bay. From shore one day,
I watched him button and tie his coat.

Siren Grieves

> *"What portions have I drunk of Siren's tears."*
> —*Shakespeare's Sonnet 119*

Bushels of grain, sheaves of wheat
bound in twine, my grief. Overhead,
seagulls squawk in sympathy
and find their way to shore.

I show them my silver belly streaks,
now stretched, now slack,
and they fly with wings that beat.
Foam on the water dies against the oars.

I am orphaned the way a marriage ends.
Look how the buoy vanishes off
the starboard side. It feels like fields,
this vast green, and sounds like wildfire,

like voices, like Siren's tears, like a floating
field combine, like a wake moving through water.

Cindy Bosley grew up in Ottumwa, Iowa, and has been writing poetry since childhood. She graduated from the Iowa Writers' Workshop in 1991. After leaving her tenured teaching job in Toledo to be an at-home parent to daughters who are regular inspirations in the form of Emma, Isabel, and Molly, Cindy Bosley also quilts and creates dollhouse miniatures.

Cindy Bosley's poetry has appeared in several academic and literary journals, and she has two essays published in a college composition textbook. One of the poems in this collection, "Siren, Jealous," was first published in *Flyway Literary Journal* under the title, "You Don't Have to Leave the Room." She's written several one-act plays for campus productions, and twice attended the Squaw Valley Community of Writers Conference in the late '80s.

Bosley gives a thankful nod of literary merit and friendship to Karen Bender, Joy Parker, Sheryl St. Germain, Leonard Kress, Carl Dietrich, Kayla Williams, Loren Gladson, Craig Combs, Shannon Smith, Hod and Pat Doering, Todd Hickman, and many others, including those of the Toledo community of poets and artists. She's been meeting with a small group of writing workshop peers in Toledo for more than 20 years.